KALEIDOSCOPE

THE WINTER AT VALLEY FORGE

by
Edward F. Dolan

BENCHMARK BOOKS

MARSHALL CAVENDISH
NEW YORK

Benchmark Books
Marshall Cavendish Corporation
99 White Plains Road
Tarrytown, New York 10591-9001
Website: www.marshallcavendish.com

Library of Congress Cataloging-in-Publication Data
Dolan, Edward F., date
The winter at Valley Forge / by Edward F. Dolan
    p.cm. – (Kaleidoscope)
Includes bibliographical references and index.
ISBN 0-7614-1304-9
1. Washington, George, 1732-1799—Headquarters—Pennsylvania—Valley Forge—Juvenile literature.
2. Valley Forge (Pa.)—History—Juvenile literature. 3. United States—History—Revolution, 1775-1783—
Juvenile literature. 4. United States. Continental Army—Military life—Juvenile literature. [1. United States—
History—Revolution, 1775-1783—Campaigns. 2. Valley Forge (Pa.)—History.] I. Title. II. Kaleidoscope
(Tarrytown, N.Y.)
E234.D65 2001   973.3'341—dc21   00-049800

Photo Research by Anne Burns Images

Cover Photo: Valley Forge Historical Society

The photographs in this book are used by permission and through the courtesy of:
Northwind Picture Archives: 10, 13, 18, 27, 41. The Bridgeman Art Library: 6.
The Granger Collection: 14, 17, 22, 25, 30, 33, 34, 37, 38, 42. Stock Montage/ SuperStock: 9, 21.
Brown Military Collection, Brown University: 29.

Printed in Italy

6 5 4 3 2 1

CONTENTS

THE FIRST SNOWS

The first snows of the year came in December, bringing the battles of 1777 to an end. The opposing armies in the American Revolutionary War tramped into their winter camps in Pennsylvania. The British settled in the city of Philadelphia. The Americans hiked over icy roads to a place called Valley Forge.

Valley Forge stood just thirteen miles from the last camp occupied by the Americans before they went into winter quarters in 1777. Because of the terrible weather, it took them an entire week to march that distance.

4

Valley Forge lay about twenty miles northwest of Philadelphia. It was a narrow valley several miles long, with the Schuylkill River running through it. A low plateau, two miles long and covered with oak and pine trees, stretched away from its eastern end. The valley was named for a blacksmith's shop that had stood there for years.

A section of land near Valley Forge was so fertile that the early settlers called it the Fat Lands of Egypt, in honor of Egypt's rich Nile Delta.

General George Washington, the commander of the American Army, watched his eleven thousand troops arrive on December 19 to make camp in the valley and on the plateau. They were a sad looking lot in ragged uniforms. Many trudged along without shoes. Their feet were wrapped in strips torn from their blankets. The strips had been ripped to shreds on the frozen roads. Washington said that anyone could have tracked his men to camp "by the blood of their feet."

General George Washington believed Valley Forge would make a fine camp, since much of it stood on a plateau that would give a broad view of the British in case of an attack.

9

On arriving, the troops built campfires. Then, exhausted, freezing, and hungry, they sat and stared into the flames. They had eaten nothing but scraps of food from their knapsacks during the march.

The Americans had fought the British all during 1777 with mixed results. They had won some battles and had lost others. Now, in the coming months, they would face a new enemy—death from hunger, disease, and the bitter cold. Only if they could fend off this new enemy could they continue to fight for their country's independence. If so, they had a chance to win. If not, the American Revolution was doomed.

On arriving at Valley Forge, the soldiers had to sit by their campfires for long hours before they could begin pitching their tents. The wagons carrying the tents had become separated from the troops during the march.

11

CAMP TAKES SHAPE

After awhile, the troops began to set up their tents. The tents were as ragged as the men's uniforms. The temperatures had dropped to freezing and the wind was a constant foe. Washington knew the tents would never last the winter. Small cabins had to be built to replace them, if the army was to survive until spring.

The worn tents provided scant shelter. The harsh winds not only shredded their thin walls, but also ripped their stakes from the ground.

13

Carrying axes, the men limped into the surrounding woods. They sent trees crashing to the ground and then cut them into boards. Small cabins slowly took shape in the next weeks, each about sixteen feet long and topped with a slanted roof. Long weeks passed before they were ready for use.

The cabins took shape slowly for two reasons. First, the men grew weaker with hunger each day. Some could work only a few minutes at a time while others collapsed as they swung their axes.

 The cabins were sixteen feet long and fourteen feet wide, and only six and a half feet high. Each had what was called a "cat-and-clay" chimney, made of clay and straw.

But why? Why were they starving when there was ample food in the young United States to feed them? It was because the food was located in distant marketplaces. When food was purchased for the troops, there were often no wagons to haul it to them. And, often, when wagons were hired, they broke down on the rough roads to the valley.

Next, they were not only short of food. They were also without the axes and other tools needed for the job—and without the clothing that would keep them warm while they worked to build the cabins.

Wagons were often in danger of breaking down on the road before they could deliver their precious cargo to the soldiers at Valley Forge.

There were reasons for the food shortage at Valley Forge. Chief among them was the demand of farmers and merchants for gold in payment for their products.

Again, why? Why were they without these things? Most Americans at that time lived by farming, with only a few of them making their living from manufacturing. Most factory goods, from uniforms and shoes to tools, were constantly in short supply.

Finally, money was always scarce. This was perhaps the worst problem of all. The Continental Congress had little to spend on the army. Further, many farmers, manufacturers, and merchants put their desire for money ahead of their loyalty to the rebels. They sold their wares only to the British, who were able to pay for them in gold.

19

DAILY LIFE
AT VALLEY FORGE

The ragged Americans struggled to stay alive through the frozen days as the year 1778 dawned. They gathered outside their cabins for roll call each morning. There, they learned of those who had died of the cold, hunger, or illness during the night. Before spring returned, one man in every four men at Valley Forge would die.

Washington visits his ragged troops with one of his officers, the marquis de Lafayette. Lafayette crossed the Atlantic Ocean at the age of twenty-one to fight for the Americans, served Washington loyally, and played a role in the final British defeat in 1781.

21

The rest of each day was spent at various chores. Men were sent to fetch water for the cabins. They carried wooden pails to the valley's Schuylkill River and dipped them into its icy waters. Then they lugged their heavy loads back to the cabins. Often, they slipped on the patches of ice on their paths. Often, their weak legs gave way beneath them. Often, they left more water on the ground than they brought home.

Musket repair was an important task throughout the winter at Valley Forge. Performing the job were men who had been gunsmiths in civilian life.

Various illnesses plagued the camp. Dysentery—a severe loosening of the bowels—spread among the men due to the unsanitary conditions. The lack of soap for washing caused rashes on their skin that itched constantly. Frozen feet led to gangrene, a condition that could be stopped only by amputation. The damp interiors of the cabins triggered infections, coughs, and chest problems.

Washington and Lafayette again visit the sick and shivering troops.

Daily, the men stood guard at various points in the camp. They were always on the watch for attacks by British patrols and for merchants trying to slip past them so that they could sell their wares to the British in Philadelphia. One sentry proudly manned his post in a tattered but clean uniform—always standing on his hat to keep his bare feet away from the snow-covered ground.

Now and again, shipments of food made their way into the valley. Wagons brought a small load of mutton at Christmas. Flour arrived from time to time. The men mixed it with water, placed it on hot stones, and cooked it into tasteless biscuits called hardtack. Someone nicknamed them "fire cakes."

A ragged and freezing sentry patiently awaits the arrival of the guard who will take his place in a few minutes.

SOME DAYS ARE GOOD

The days were bleak and cold. But there were some pleasant moments, too. In early 1778, General Washington's wife, Martha, came to stay with her husband at the farmhouse that served as his headquarters. Every day, she toured the valley, visiting the soldiers and passing out bits of food from a basket.

Martha Washington is welcomed by her husband. She and General Washington occupied a gray stone house belonging to Isaac Potts, the man who owned the forge that gave the valley its name.

Early 1778 brought another addition to Valley Forge—the stout and red-faced Friedrich von Steuben of Germany. He was a veteran soldier who had sailed to America to join the fight against the British. He proved to be one of the most important officers ever at the winter camp.

He proved important because he had heard that the Americans were good fighters but that they lacked military training and discipline. They were excellent marksmen but took too long to load and fire their muskets. They were fine fighters but often did not move together or obey orders fast enough to win in battle. They often ignored or disobeyed an order if they disliked it. These problems had cost Washington's army many lives and victories. He decided to correct them.

Baron Friedrich von Steuben walks with George Washington as they tour Valley Forge. Before joining the American cause, von Steuben served as an officer in the army of Prussia. He also served on the military staff of Frederick the Great, the founder of modern Germany.

Puffing in the icy air, von Steuben set about training the men daily. He taught them how to load and fire their muskets in half the time they usually took. He coached them in military discipline and courtesy. He had them practice close order drill for hours. In so doing, he taught them an all-important lesson: in the victorious army, all the men are able to move, obey orders, and fight together with great speed, as if they were a single person.

Though he was a hard taskmaster, the men loved and admired the shouting von Steuben. He worked them hard, yes. But he worked himself just as hard. They grinned as he sweated and yelled his orders in a mixture of German, French, and a few English swear words that he had picked up.

Baron von Steuben began his training program with one hundred American soldiers. They in turn trained their comrades while he worked with another set of soldiers.

34

His teachings slowly took root through the long weeks to spring, spreading from the lowliest private to the highest-ranking officer. When the winter ended, the troops were better soldiers, more efficient than ever been before. They were disciplined. They acted swiftly together. Von Steuben's lessons would serve them well in coming battles and would be passed on to future generations of American soldiers.

Because of his teachings, the old warrior von Steuben was to go down in history as the father of the United States army.

 The baron remained in the Army until 1784. He then retired to live in New York State. He remained deeply interested in military affairs for the rest of his life, and championed the formation of a national military academy.

AS SPRING APPROACHES

Life at Valley Forge improved as spring drew near. Wagons containing bolts of cloth lumbered into camp one morning. Soldiers who had once been tailors hurried from their cabins with scissors, needles, and thread. Soon, new uniforms were to be seen everywhere.

At the same time, soldiers began obtaining shoes through trading with the local farmers. Until then, some 2500 men had been without any footwear at all.

Many of the soldiers stole away from Valley Forge during the winter to help their families at home. When spring came, most of their number returned to camp.

The food shortage was also solved in the passing weeks. Food shipments of varying amounts arrived. Then the Schuylkill River itself ended the shortage. Its waters began to churn as though struck by a wild wind. But the air was still. Rather, the river was alive with thousands of fish called shad, making their spring run along its course.

Soldiers plunged into the churning waters with pitchforks and shovels. They snared the fish and hurled them up on the banks, where the catch was immediately cooked and eaten. There was enough left over to salt and preserve for future use. Hunger at Valley Forge disappeared.

With the coming of spring, the annual shad run along the Schuylkill River helped to end the food shortage at Valley Forge.

The stay at Valley Forge ended in June 1778 when Washington ordered the troops to go in search of the enemy. Since December, the tide had turned for his army. His men, thanks to von Steuben, were now disciplined soldiers. They would be more effective in battle than ever before. The months of suffering had hardened their resolve to go on fighting. Best of all, a major European power had taken up their cause. France had recently announced that it was joining America in the fight against the British.

Under the direction of George Washington, the troops at Valley Forge went on to defeat the British. Washington would eventually become the first president of the United States.

41

Another great American revolutionary, Benjamin Franklin, sits with his fellow diplomats at the signing of the Peace Treaty of Paris in September 1783, which effectively ended the Revolutionary War.

With French help, Washington's men would now fight on. Ahead of them were three years of warfare that would take the opposing armies to the city of Yorktown in Virginia. There, the British would finally surrender on October 19, 1781, opening the way to peace negotiations that would bring the Revolutionary War to a formal close with the signing of the Treaty of Paris on September 3, 1783.

TIMELINE

1777 December, fighting ends for the year. The American Army makes its winter camp at Valley Forge, Pennsylvania.

1778 Life at Valley Forge is marked by freezing weather, hunger and illness.

Martha Washington comes to stay at Valley Forge.

Friedrich von Steuben, a veteran German soldier, arrives and turns the American army into disciplined fighters.

June. The stay at Valley Forge ends. The Americans, newly allied with the French, return to war.

1781 The British surrender at Yorktown, Virginia in October.

1783 The American Revolutionary War formally ends when the Treaty of Paris is signed on September 3rd.

FIND OUT MORE

BOOKS:

Busch, Noel. *Winter Quarters: George Washington and the Continental Army at Valley Forge.* New York: Liveright, 1974.

Fleming, Thomas J. *First in Their Hearts: A Biography of George Washington.* New York: W.W. Norton, 1968.

Lancaster, Bruce. *From Lexington to Liberty: The Story of the American Revolution.* Garden City, NY: Doubleday, 1955.

Reed, John F. *Valley Forge: Crucible of Victory.* Monmouth, NJ: Phililp Freneau Press, 1969.

Stein, R. Conrad. *Valley Forge.* Chicago: Children's Press, 1994.

WEBSITES:

Historic Valley Forge
http://www.ushistory.org/valleyforge/index.html

Virtual Marching Tour of the American Revolution
http://www.ushistory.org/march/index.html

Historic Valley Forge: Martha Washington
http://www.ushistory.org/valleyforge/served/martha.html

AUTHOR'S BIO

Edward F. Dolan is the author of over one hundred nonfiction books for young people and adults. He has written on medicine and science, law, history, folklore, and current social issues. Mr. Dolan is a native Californian, born in the San Francisco region and raised in Southern California. In addition to writing books, he has been a newspaper reporter and a magazine editor. He currently lives in the northern part of the state.

INDEX

Page numbers for illustrations are in boldface.